BROTHERLY LOVE

CARL M. MOORE

PROMINENT
BOOKS

5830 E 2nd St, Ste 7000 #9983
Casper, WY 82609
USA

UPPER NORTH

NORTHEAST

WEST

NORTH

CENTER CITY

SOUTHWEST

SOUTH

Philadelphia
philadelphia

PHILADELPHIA

As you see the cover of my book, you see the picture of the city hall. City Hall is right at the center of the city itself. I looked back and thought, "What was so special about that city of Philadelphia?" Well, during my time, here was the list of what would pop up in my mind:

1. Good places to visit in downtown (center city) of Philadelphia would be the following:

   A. City Hall / Independence Hall / Liberty Bell Center
   B. Betsy Ross House where the thirteen stars of America's old Bag were made.
   C. Museum of Art / Franklin Mint
   D. Chinese town
   E. Waterfront / Penn's Landing
   F. The Gallery (mall)
   G. Central Club for the Deaf (no longer there)

2. Good places to visit in North Philadelphia (Philly) would be the following:

    A. Temple University (TU)
    B. Joe Frazier's Gym
    C. Philadelphia Phillies (baseball team)
    D. Zoo (animal park)
    E. W. & E. Martin School for the Hearing Impaired
    F. White/Hispanic/Black communities

3. Good places to visit in Northeast Philadelphia would be the following:

    A. Internal Revenue Service (IRS)
    B. Silent Athletic Club (SAC)
    C. Jewish/Catholic/White communities

4. Good places to visit in Upper North (Northwest) Philadelphia would be the following:

    A. Germantown
    B. Pennsylvania School for the Deaf (PSD)
    C. Roxborough High School
    D. White/Black communities

5. Good places to visit in West Philadelphia (Philly) would be the following:

    A. Thirtieth Street Station (train)
    B. United States Post Office

C. University City / Drexel Hill University / University of Penn

D. Elwyn Institutes

E. George Brooks Elementary School

F. Asian/White/Black communities

6. Good places to visit in South Philadelphia (Philly) would be the following:

   A. Philadelphia Airport

   B. Philadelphia Eagles (football team)

   C. Philadelphia Flyers (hockey team)

   D. Philadelphia 76ers (basketball team)

   E. South Street / Italian / Hispanic / Black communities

7. Famous people:

   A. Bill Cosby (comedian)

   B. Joe Frazier (boxer)

   C. Mayor Rizzo

   D. Dr. J (basketball player)

   E. Wilt Chamberlain (basketball player)

   F. Charles Barkley (basketball player)

   G. Reggie White (football player)

   H. Bobby Clarke (hockey player)

8. Famous foods/dessert:

    A. Italian hoagies
    B. Cheesesteak
    C. Sweet potato pies

GOAL IN LIFE

To work hard or study hard is the best way to escape boredom or become a successful person.

Learn how to handle stress at work.

Study and ask for help when needed.

Parents get involved when needed.

This book is dedicated to my parents, Rev. Carl A. Moore and Mrs. Naomi Moore, who taught me how to overcome the challenges I encountered in my life, in my disability, in my education, in my home environment, and in my work.

CONTENTS

- West Philadelphia in the Black Community
- George Brooks Elementary School in 1958
- Walk
- Communication problem
- W. & E. Martin School for the Hearing Impaired from 1958 to 1968
- North Philadelphia in the White Community
- Ride on the bus
- Black English vs. English problem
- Vocational vs. Academic
- Speech Therapy / Audio Training
- Masterman Junior High School for Math and Science Only
- Upper Northwest Philadelphia in the White Community
- Roxborough High School from 1968 to 1971
- Rode on Public Transportation
- Major in Commercial Academic / Member of the National Honor Society
- Participated in Sports after School

  1. Bowling team for three years
  2. Chess captain of the team in second place in the city of Philadelphia
  3. Soccer team for about two years
  4. Track team

ACKNOWLEDGMENT

I WANT TO acknowledge and thank my brother, Henry "Hank" Moore, who taught me about Black English in our home environment within the Black community while we were growing up in West Philadelphia, Pennsylvania.

FOREWORD BY DR. JERRY DRENNAN

THIS IS A manuscript that most of us have attempted to write…either on paper, orally, or mentally. Any effort to explain, clarify, justify, or simply share "ourself" is a daunting exercise. The author is to be commended for this document.

Carl is uniquely qualified to present himself to us. He is a representative from a family of deaf and hearing members. He has successfully experienced the "deaf world" and the "hearing world."

Carl's educational and professional career spans the world of public and private education. He has worked in service opportunities of the government, religious service and ministry, and continues to serve both the hearing and the deaf communities in his later life.

Dr. Jerry Drennan
Abilene, Texas

FOREWORD BY DR. FRED BOGAN

FOR APPROXIMATELY TEN years, I assisted Carl Moore as he pastored one of the largest and most successful deaf ministries in the country right here in Tulsa, Oklahoma. I was always amazed at his patience and diligence when working with the deaf members of our congregation. However, in all that time, we never really discussed Carl's early life and the many circumstances that guided him to make the life decisions that he did.

We did know that Carl had significant training and experience in psychological counseling, and it showed when he worked with people. We were truly blessed to have Carl as our minister for that many years. He was so much better with the deaf community than anyone else around that we leaned heavily on him as our liaison for the deaf. In his book *Brotherly Love*, we learn things about Carl that we never would have learned any other way. Thank you for that, Carl. Thank you also for ten wonderful years of great shepherding of our deaf community here in Tulsa.

Dr. Fred Bogan
Park Church of Christ
Tulsa, Oklahoma

This author used the Holy Bible Easy to Read Version (ERV). Also, this author wanted to show you with three main points of his story from his personal experiences and/or obstacles. So, this book will tell us the following:

1. God has a reason for all of the problems that we faced.
2. God made a plan for you.
3. God has given this day to you.

PREFACE

First of all, I want to thank you, my readers. My book is a true story of my life. I hope that my book will help you to understand where I came from, what my life was like in the Philadelphia, Pennsylvania, which is called the "City of Brotherly Love," and how I overcame with my disability.

INTRODUCTION

——

THIS WAS A story about a boy who was born Black and deaf, and he was raised in the city of brotherly love in Philadelphia, Pennsylvania. His name is Carl "Mike" Moore.

CHAPTER 1

Bible Reading

Bible Reading:

A. Mark 12:28–34 (ERV)

Which Command Is the Most Important?

ONE OF THE teachers of the law came to Jesus. He heard Jesus arguing with the Sadducees and the Pharisees. He saw that Jesus gave good answers to their questions. So he asked him, "Which of the commands is the most important?"

Jesus answered, "The most important command is this: 'People of Israel, listen! The Lord our God is the only Lord. Love the Lord your God with all your heart, all your soul, all your mind, and all your strength.' The second most important command is this: 'Love your neighbor the same as you love yourself.' These two commands are the most important."

The man answered, "That was a good answer, Teacher. You are right in saying that God is the only Lord and that there is no other God. And you must love God with all your heart, all your mind, and all your strength. And you must love others the same as you love yourself. These commands are more important than all the animals and sacrifices we offer to God."

Jesus saw that the man answered him wisely. So he said to him, "You are close to God's kingdom." And after that time, no one was brave enough to ask Jesus any more questions.

Bible Reading:
B. Genesis 50:15–21 (ERV)

The Brothers Are Still Afraid of Joseph

After Jacob died, Joseph's brothers were worried. They were afraid that Joseph would still be mad at them for what they had done years before. They said, "Maybe Joseph still hates us for what we did." So the brothers sent this message to Joseph:

"Before your father died, he told us to give you a message. He said, 'Tell Joseph that I beg him to please forgive his brothers for the bad things they did to him.' So now Joseph, we beg you, please forgive us for the bad things we did to you. We are the servants of God, the God of your father."

That message made Joseph very sad, and he cried. His brothers went to him and bowed down in front of him. They said, "We will be your servants."

Then Joseph said to them, "Don't be afraid. I am not God! I have no right to punish you. It is true that you planned to do something bad to me. But really, God was planning good things. God's plan was to use me to save the lives of many people. And that is what happened. So don't be afraid. I will take care of you and your children." And so Joseph said kind things to his brothers, and this made them feel better.

CHAPTER 2

What Was Mike's Family Like?

HIS FATHER WAS a minister, and he was a hearing person. His mother was a housewife, and she was an oral/deaf person. They had seven children. Mike was the second oldest of seven children.

Carl and His Family

Born in Philadelphia, Pennsylvania, Carl is Black and deaf. And he is proud of it. But he has not always felt that way. His father, who was hearing, had been a longshoreman for many years and has since become a Baptist minister. His mother, who is oral/hard of hearing, has worked for the Internal Revenue Service for many years. Carl is second oldest of seven children—three hearing and four deaf. Carl's oldest sister was born normal. Later, she had an illness that caused her to become hard of hearing. Carl was congenitally deaf, but he did not know what caused it. According to his mother, the doctor did not know why. So, the doctor reported that the cause of his deafness was unknown. Next to Carl was his hearing brother and sister. Next to them was Carl's deaf sister. Next to her was Carl's hearing sister. Last one was Carl's hard-of-hearing sister. Carl believed that it was a strong possibility that he and his sisters with hearing loss were because of his mother. Carl's family communicated each other by speech only. His family also stressed only oral method.

Carl and His Early Education

Carl began his education at George Brooks Elementary School in West Philadelphia, Pennsylvania. As he recalled, he could remember that he was at approximately age of five. All of his classmate and the teacher were hearing. He noticed that he was different by the way they treated him. Somehow, the principal discovered Carl's problem, and he was transferred to an oral school. The oral/

day school was called W. & E. Martin School for the Hearing Impaired. This oral/ day school was located in the White community of North Philadelphia. Carl could not forget because they were many children like him. Many of those children wore hearing aids. Carl did not wear hearing aid until he was about six and a half years old. As he grew up, he studied and learned speaking, lipreading, and other regular subjects that any young elementary school child would take. While Carl was in this oral/day school for almost ten years, he and the students were not allowed to use sign language. Carl has seen the other type of deaf students from the Pennsylvania School for the Deaf at the public places. While Carl watched those deaf students used their sign language to communicate with each other, Carl knew that he could not communicate with them. More so, Carl shied away from them. Even more so, Carl did not want hearing people to know that he was also deaf.

Carl and His Communication

Carl's communication at school progressed. But at home, Carl had problems before the recorder for the television, interpreter for the deaf, doorbell light, special clock, telecommunication device for the deaf, and other devices that were available to his family. Carl did not know about it. Communication was always his problem. For instance, when his family get a phone call, he always has to be left out of their conservation. When his family was watching the TV, Carl would ask what it was saying. He usually received an answer like, "It is not important" or "I don't know."

When his relatives come to visit his family, he could not follow their conversation. He always felt frustrated. So, he understood that he had to live that way for the rest of his life. Sometimes, his family would let him know what the television, telephone, and conversations with others are about.

Furthermore, in the Black community, Carl realized that the culture and language were different from what he learned from his oral/ day school in the White community. At home, his hearing brother, who is one and a half years younger than him, helped him a lot by teaching him how to speak in Black English or slang, how to play different games, and how to go around to the stores, libraries, playgrounds, etc. But Carl did not like it when he learned that his parents always wanted his brother to go with him everywhere.

Finally, he escaped from his brother to prove to his parents that he could become independent. Although Carl's mother and he could managed well, he could never quite "tune into" his father. He meant that he could not understand his father's feelings very well. Carl always felt that the church and religion were the center of activity of his father, his family, and other Black families in their community. He was confused, often moved, and wondered what was being said.

Carl and His Education

At oral/day school, Carl continued to study and work hard. He rode to oral/ day school and home by school bus during the weekdays. He tried to prove that he was just as important and smart as his hearing brother and sisters. But sometimes the more he learned, the less he felt he could understand. He was told by his Black friends that he was too ambitious. White children told him he was too different, that he was dirty. Carl scrubbed his body from head to toe, and still they would not accept him because they said black skin was always dirty. Carl was confused and hurt. And somewhere, down deep, he was getting angry.

The "streets" offered another kind of education. Carl chased girls, raced, played daredevil games, and fought. He was sometimes cornered by neighborhood bullies, and he would hand over his money and hope his parents would not find out. And then he would wonder even more what his world was about.

Language was a constant challenge for Carl. In addition to the basic language acquisition problems associated with his deafness, Carl was faced with the Black English used by most of his friends. This added a whole new dimension to his communication development. When should he use what? Which was correct?

Carl and His First Employment

At the age of thirteen, Carl was stopped by a man in a car and asked if he wanted a job as a newspaper boy. Carl read his lip and said yes. This man took Carl home, and he talked with Carl's parents. First, Carl's parents did not like the idea. While they were talking, Carl was watching and hoping his parents would change their minds. Somehow, they agreed that Carl could have the job if his brother would work with him. Then Carl and his brother worked on one newspaper route together.

Later, his brother stopped working, and Carl took the whole route. It did not last because his family moved to a better neighborhood. Later, Carl got another job through his hard-of-hearing classmate where his hard-of-hearing classmate's mother worked at the laboratory. Carl and his classmate worked as mail clerks during the weekdays after school and sometimes on weekend.

Carl Graduated

When Carl graduated from W. & E. Martin School for the Hearing Impaired in 1968, Carl entered Roxborough High School where he was on his own. There were no special services for the deaf. Carl studied and worked hard and tried to overcome the stereotype of vocational training for Black and deaf people. He wanted the academic track. He knew that he could become "someone" through education. His mother encouraged him with this idea. After school, he participated in sports: bowling, chess, soccer, and track.

Carl and His Challenges

All during the sixties, when civil rights and Black militancy and Black awareness were growing, Carl was minimally affected because he had so many immediate, everyday concerns, let alone the things in the newspapers and on television.

Carl also realized that his school years were dominated by Whites while his home life was dominated by Blacks. So, having been raised and educated in oral and regular public schools, Carl has had the advantage of learning to master both the Black English spoken by the Black community and the standard English spoken by the White community.

Carl had the advantages of not only developing his language skills, but also learning what life is all about. But there were also disadvantages. One disadvantage of being raised as an oralist is that of not having the opportunity to ask questions. You learned things without knowing why you were learning them. So, Carl had a lot of questions. He needed explanations. He needed guidance.

Carl Graduated from High School

Fortunately, Carl is a fighter. He decided that he would demand answers. He decided he would not accept less just because he was Black, deaf, and had less money than most of his friends. That drive, that desire to achieve, guided him through Roxborough High School where he graduated with honors and went on to Rochester Institute of Technology/ National Technical Institute for the Deaf (RIT/NTID) in Rochester, New York.

Carl and His Employment History

Before going to college, Carl also worked at the car wash during his three years of high school. He worked there as a car wash finisher. He worked on weekends and in the summers. Between the ages of thirteen and nineteen, Carl worked on various jobs such as a newspaper boy, mail clerk, and car wash finisher. Those jobs taught him how to be responsible and get along with others. At the same time, Carl learned that living with his family was important to him because he experienced a good family relationship and a sense of belonging even though he had communication problems, fewer close friendship with classmates from oral and hearing schools, and less social interaction with his deaf peers.

Carl and His College Education

Carl chose Rochester Institute of Technology/National Technical Institute for the Deaf (RIT/ NTID) at that time because it offered the two worlds of the hearing and the deaf all on one campus. But once he arrived at NTID, Carl did not want to have anything to do with the deaf people.

"Somehow," he recalled, "I didn't really consider myself deaf. I specially shied away from sign language so hearing people wouldn't be able to spot me. Finally, I realized that I was doing what others had always done to me as a Black person."

Once Carl learned to approach each person as an individual, "a whole new life—a new world—opened for me," he related.

During the summer of 1971 at NTID, Carl also learned sign language and decided to major in accounting. One year later, Carl changed his major to business technology (office practice and procedure).

Carl Graduated from College

After Carl finished NTID in December 1973, he graduated in June 1974 with an associate degree in office practice and procedure. He went to work on various types of jobs. He was a control clerk in Pennsylvania, dietary aide and dishwasher in Virginia, and clerk-typist in Washington, DC, within the first eight months of 1974.

Finally, Carl found a well-paying position with the Philadelphia Post Office as a distribution clerk. While he worked there for three years, he usually slept in the mornings. Afternoons and off-days were spent with his family or involved in some aspect of the deaf community. He attended meetings, workshops, conferences, and parties within the local deaf society. Some of his activities were helping deaf individuals with their wants, needs, and problems. For instance, Carl became president of the Black Deaf Association to help others like himself live a better life.

Carl and the Newspaper

On Wednesday, May 11, 1977, Carl was interviewed by Alfonso D. Brown, Jr., of the *Evening Bulletin* staff. The title was "Silent World Has Prejudices— Black Deaf Group Fights for Equality." According to this article, it stated, "Carl Moore— fighting all my life." More so, it stated, "Carl Moore is deaf and Black and as the president of the Black Deaf Association, a 490-member group, he is trying to help others like himself live a better life.

"Even the silent world has it's prejudices," said the twenty-five-year-old West Oak Lane man. "Deaf Blacks have to fight so they can be equal. I've been fighting all my life." Moore said deaf Blacks are deprived in health, education, economics and social life. "Deaf Blacks don't get a good education."

Moore said, "People feel they aren't as smart as the others. In many cases, they don't have the money and in others, they aren't given the chance."

Another problem facing them is finding out what services are available. Moore said it's difficult for them to find where to go for help. "We don't know what's happening to the deaf community," he said.

"The unemployment rate among deaf Black males is five times greater than that of deaf White males," Moore said. "More jobs are needed," Moore said, adding that deaf persons are underpaid.

"This should be stopped," he said. "Deaf persons are always the first to get laid off," he said.

Moore said a main function of the association is to let others know their special needs. "We are telling other deaf organizations what we want. We need a deaf Black program," he said.

Moore will be speaking at the White House Conference on Handicapped Individuals in Washington, DC, from May 23 through 26.

Governor Shapp has selected Moore to represent the state's eighty thousand deaf persons at the conference.

Moore said, however, he'll be representing the entire state and any deaf person wanting to offer suggestions for the conference can contact him.

Some suggestions Moore will be making to officials are reduced telephone-teletype rates for the deaf and more teletype machines.

The teletype is a special machine used by deaf persons to communicate over the telephone. It prints words so the deaf person can read the message and know what the other person has said.

Moore is also asking for more television programming for the deaf, equal access to public transportation and handicapped persons, special tax benefits and more courtroom interpreters.

He also said insurance companies discriminate against the deaf by charging higher auto insurance rates. "Statistics show that deaf drivers have fewer accidents than those who can hear. Yet, we pay more to drive," Moore stated.

At the conference in 1977, Carl spoke on a racial issue. His special concern was about the Black deaf group as a minority and their rights. Carl liked to quote from his Councilman Lucien E. Blackwell: "My Polish colleagues, my Jewish colleague, my Italian colleagues—it is all right for them to discuss their ethnic background. So why is it wrong for me to discuss the problems of the Blacks? Matter-of-factly, we Blacks have all the problems, and we need special attention. There is nothing racist about that."

Governor Shapp, in his letter to Mr. Carl Moore, stated, "Your demonstrated knowledge, leadership, and concern for those citizens who are handicapped make you a good advocate for the Commonwealth of Pennsylvania. I know there are hundreds of Pennsylvanians who are looking to you for leadership and help appropriate changes for the disabled of our state and country."

Carl felt that being Black and deaf was not easy. He said that he had two major problems that he was Black and deaf. He was quite aware of his problems by writing about things, persons, and others that he felt writing these communications was a wonderful way to organize his own thinking. He said this was no reason why you couldn't try for yourself. Another reasons that Carl was quite aware of his problems was that he had experience in deaf schools, hearing schools, and college. He grew up a Black deaf person with many problems.

Carl received congratulations and best wishes on his appointment by the Governor to the White House Conference on Handicapped Individuals from Secretary of the Commonwealth, C. Delores Tucker.

Carl was married and has two sons. And he worked as a clerk for the United Postal Services at night. His past activities were the following:

1. Assistant director, Society for Helping Church, Inc.
2. Board of director, Deafness and Hearing Impairment Council of Southeastern Pennsylvania
3. Member of Nevil Communications Project Committee
4. President pro tem, Greater Philadelphia Federation of Organizations of the Deaf
5. Member, Philadelphia Silent Athletic Club
6. Member, Central Philadelphia Silent Club
7. Member, Delaware Valley Tele-Communications for the Deaf
8. Board of director, Southeastern Pennsylvania Legal Services for the Deaf
9. Member, Roxborough High School Alumni
10. Member, Rochester Institute of Technology/National Technical Institute for the Deaf Alumni
11. Lifetime member, Pennsylvania Society for the Advancement of the Deaf (PSAD)

As result of this community work with the deaf, Carl realized that he wanted to do even more for the deaf people. He knew that he needed a more complete education for this, so he decided to attend Gallaudet College in January 1978. Even though he had already attended NTID and received an AAS degree from there, he thought Gallaudet would be a better place to pursue social work. The program is strong at Gallaudet, and it would be a good experience to meet new people.

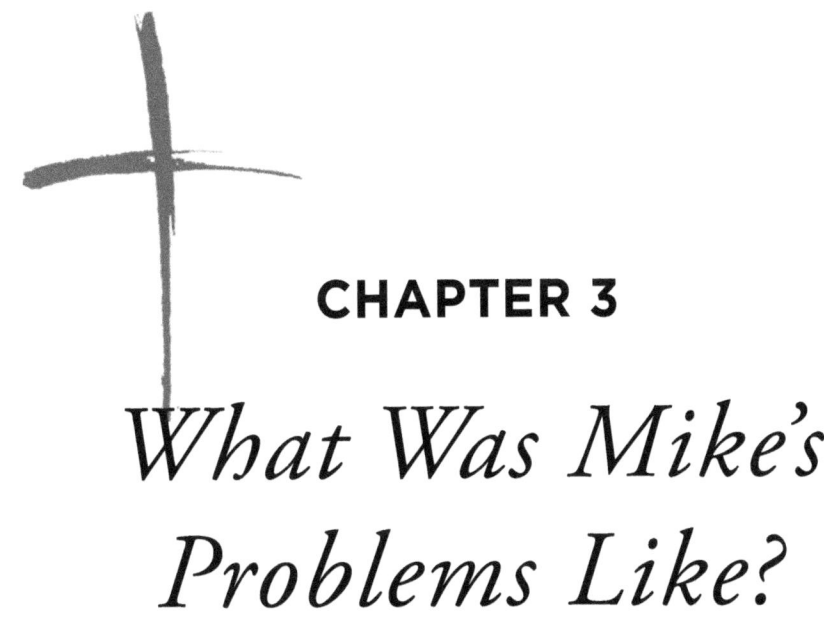

CHAPTER 3

What Was Mike's Problems Like?

MIKE GREW UP with many problems and questions. For example, his questions were like:

- Why did my younger hearing brother talk a lot with my father?
- Why did my older hard-of-hearing sister talk a lot with my mother?
- Why did I have to take so many whips?
- Why did my brother and my parents make my life difficult?
- Why didn't my parents understand me?
- How did I become deaf?
- Why did my neighbors have to make fun of me and my family?
- Why did my friends(s) pick on me?
- Why was I alone a lot?
- Why was I confused?

Other than that, during his time, in between 1958 and 1971, Mike remembered that his family had no special devices for the deaf such as doorbell, telephone, etc. He often watched black-and-white television with no closed caption. He tried to understand what was happened outside of his home during the civil rights era. More so, Mike considered himself fortunate to have been raised in a family in which his hearing father and deaf mother did their best in instill a sense of self-worth in their children.

By observing the discrimination his father, a minister and longshoreman, faced. Mike came to understand the price that many Blacks had to pay to be accepted as full American citizens. Also, he observed that his deaf mother, who was raised orally, kept up with her children's academic progress, often speaking out against the injustices in the educational system. Although Mike's parents did raise their family well, he remembered that he used to walk to school at George Brooks Elementary School in West Philadelphia.

Eventually, he was transferred to the Martin School for the Hearing Impaired in North Philadelphia in the White community. Then he had to ride on the school bus. At the Martin School (oral/ day school), he would learn how to speak and listen in English language along with academic course work.

CHAPTER 4

What Led Mike to the Complete Acceptance of Both His Black and Deaf Cultures?

FIRST OF ALL, Mike praised his mother for knowing what to do. For years, he traveled and told his inspiring story at times of his preadulthood inner struggle that finally led him to the complete acceptance of both Black and Deaf cultures.

CHAPTER 5

How Did Mike Overcome His Problems?

So, at age nineteen, Mike realized a self-fulfilling joining of the two cultures. In a society where the issues of minorities and deaf children are at the bottom of the political agenda, Mike and other Black deaf leaders across the country stand as advocates and role models for both the Black community and the Deaf community. Before his father died, Mike grew up, learned, and realized that his father knew a lot about Black culture, but not Deaf culture. So, again, Mike forged ahead by accepted both Black culture and Deaf culture. Today, Mike is proud to be a member of both cultures. More so, Mike proudly said, "Blackness and deafness equals knowledge and respect of Black and Deaf culture."

CONCLUSION

———◦———◦———

IN OUR RECENT Bible reading, it tells us to remember Joseph's words when he spoke to his brothers. Joseph said that God turned something bad into something good. God had a reason for all of the problems that we faced. Yes, it may be hard for all of us to understand God's plan, but someday we will understand. So, don't be discouraged today. God has given this day to you. You have an opportunity to serve Him today. Keep on focusing on God. He will also help you to overcome any of your problems that you may have today.

IN MEMORY

My beloved brother, Henry "Hank" Moore, who just recently passed away on
September 15, 2020

ABOUT THE AUTHOR

CARL WAS BORN and raised in Philadelphia, Pennsylvania, to a deceased hearing father and deceased deaf mother. He is the second oldest of seven children (three hearing and four deaf). Carl and his wife, Nina, were married in 1998 and have four grown children. Although Carl is originally from Philadelphia, Pennsylvania, he has lived many places.

He is a graduate of the following: National Technical Institute for the Deaf/Rochester Institute of Technology (NTID/RIT) with AAS degree in business technology ('74), Gallaudet University (GU) with BA degree in social work ('81), New York University (NYU) with MA degree in deafness rehabilitation ('83). He also holds a certificate of ordination and certification in biblical and deaf ministry studies in May 2007 and a BA degree in biblical and deaf ministry studies in May 2009. He is a lifetime member of the Pennsylvania Society for the Advancement of the Deaf (PSAD).

www.ingramcontent.com/pod-product-compliance
Lightning Source LLC
Chambersburg PA
CBHW041126120626
46547CB00019B/2869